Whisper Mountain

Vivian Higginbotham Nichols

After all these long years, the Ozark Mountains still whisper the secrets of our dead.

CONTENTS

ACKNOWLEDGMENTS

I would like to thank my father, Maurice Higginbotham, for instilling his love of family, history, writing, and this great nation. If it had not been for the fact that he had saved all of his mother's photos, letters, and legal documents, my grandmother's story would have been buried with her.

I would also like to thank my mother, Edna Higginbotham, who instilled her love for God and who was generous enough to give me Grandma's documents that allowed me to write her story. My sister, Linda, also helped with ancestry research.

I am especially indebted to my daughter, Crystal, for the countless hours she helped me in the early years of this project. Without her critique and feedback, this story would not be the same.

This incredible true story is dedicated to my grandmother, Ida Williams Higginbotham, who left us her handwritten journals, composed over a 20 year period, of the events that shaped her tragic, young life. In them she wrote that she wished she were "a storybook writer" so she could tell her story. Despite only having finished third grade, she did just that. Not only did she leave us well over 100 pages, she also kept photographs, letters, and a few legal documents that verified what she told us. She died in 1967 when I was in junior-high.

Thirty years after she passed, we inherited her huge trunk that contained all of these treasures. In them we found so many answers to questions we had about some of those events and understood why she never mentioned the names of those involved. We initially assumed she didn't know. Thankfully, she told us through her written accounts. This is her story.

Ida Williams
19 years-old
1910

1

The catalyst for the events that happened during my childhood actually began years prior to me being knitted in my mother's womb. No one can be hurt as much as I have been during my life. The bark of the tree needs to be shaved off, and let the chips fly and fall where they may. My story is from feeling and seeing things, from angels to witches, and from riches to poverty. The events that unfolded two decades before I was born only set in motion the things my siblings and I had to suffer many years later.

My grandfather, William Hamilton "John" Blackwell's parents had come over to Virginia from England. As a young boy he lived with his parents, two brothers, Jud and Hamilton, and two sisters. They later migrated to Georgia where they owned and operated a gold mine. I am not certain if they homesteaded the property with the mine or purchased it outright. Either way, they became wealthy from their efforts.

In 1820 when John was already of marriageable age, he wed a woman by the name of Sarah "Catherine." They homesteaded a section of land between Waldron and Boles, Arkansas. Their union produced five children: four sons and one daughter. I do not know all of their names, but I do remember that one was named Andrew and another Jim, who later died from dropsy. Their youngest son was named Moses. Their only daughter passed away at an early age. Catherine later died in 1851.

Andrew moved into Oklahoma where the town of Blackwell was named after him. One of John's older sons was shot and killed while sitting in a chair inside his house because his dad didn't want him to fight in the War for Southern Independence. My mother remembered seeing the hole in the wall when she was a child.

The Yankees came down onto his homestead and fought a fierce, bloody battle. The bush whackers were robbing people and threatened to hang John if he didn't give them his money. He finally gave up $1700. His brother Hamilton was shot and killed on a foot log while crossing Buffalo Creek. He was either on his way to bury his gold or had already buried it. Whether the bushwhackers got the gold or not remains a mystery.

John's youngest son, Moses, was a teenager when my grandmother Nancy first met them. Nancy was married to a Mr. T. J. Pierce and living in Missouri near her parents, the Prices. Her husband was a Confederate soldier who had gone off to fight in the war. When she got word that he had been killed in a battle on the Blackwell homestead down in Arkansas, she went to retrieve his body and give him a proper Christian burial, but she was unable to locate his body or find its whereabouts. That is when she first met John and his son.

Broken-hearted, she made her way to Hot Wells, which was later renamed Hot Springs. John had advised her that it was a two-day journey and that she should stop at Mt. Ida for the night. He told her how he had named that mountain after his Aunt Ida who at the time lived in England. I was told years later that I was named after that mountain.

In order to earn money, Nancy and some of her neighbors butchered hogs and scalded their hides in the hot water coming from the wells. With no man around to help, she lived a hard life until John Blackwell came courting. This woman stirred him from the moment he laid eyes on her, and he could not get her out of his mind. Eventually, the two fell in love and married in 1865.

Because they saw an opportunity in the town of Hot Springs, they made plans to build a bathhouse. John sold his homestead, and they purchased 440 square lots in a township of land that included the hot wells. It was not long before Nancy became pregnant with my mother. Since she desired to give birth in her hometown and the war had just come to an end, the three of them traveled back to Missouri to be with Nancy's parents. That is when my mother, Laura, was born at Willow Springs on June 16, 1866.

When Laura was three months old, they decided to move back to Hot Springs and build the bathhouse. They had a business partner, Mr. Cummins, I believe, who lived at Little Rock and put up the money, while my grandparents put up the property. The bathhouse was opened for business and quite successful. The next few years Laura spent a lot of time playing with the Cummins' daughter who was about her age. Her friend was later referred to as the "Little Rock Heiress."

In those days people believed that if you bathed in the mineral waters, it would cure you of many ailments. Consequently, floods of people from all over the country -- and even other parts of the world -- began pouring into town to take advantage of this resort. Its fame spread quickly. Even though business was booming, John and Nancy still had other pressing matters to take care of. For one, there was no school in town, so they made plans to send Laura to school in Little Rock when she was old enough to attend via the Iron Mountain Railroad line that ran close to their house.

Moses was a young man by that time and met Mary, the daughter of Mr. and Mrs. Hobbs. They fell in love and married. That is when all the trouble began. The Hobbses saw an opportunity to involve themselves in their newly acquired son-in-law's family's business, so their scheming began. They volunteered their services to help run the bathhouse, but needless to say, helping them was not their plan.

Mrs. Hobbs forced her way into taking charge of things, and she did not get along with Nancy at all. Naturally, Nancy resented the fact that this woman was trying to run their family business. Mr. and Mrs. Hobbs would ridicule the fact that little Laura, an "heiress to the resort" was born in such a small place as Willow Springs. Sarcastic remarks were common from them. Mrs. Hobbs would talk about how Laura had been raised in a cornfield, which was not even true. In the first place, what difference did any of that make?

Since there seemed to be continual conflict, John told Nancy to just let Mrs. Hobbs run the bathhouse so they could all live in peace like a family should. One day when my grandfather was working on a water gate, two of the Hobbs' sons rode up and invited him over for supper that night. My mother was five at the time and was sitting near her dad and watching the water run down over the rocks. It gave her great pleasure spending time with her dad along the springs. John assumed the Hobbses wanted to patch up their differences and be friends, so he took their invitation, but he took Laura home first.

When he arrived at the Hobbses,' they had his plate of food ready and waiting. As soon as he had eaten, he knew something was wrong. Their two sons came in and asked if he had eaten it. The boys knew their mother had put strychnine in his plate, then the food on top of it. Realizing he had been poisoned, John quickly rode home and told Nancy what had happened and told her he was very sick.

He suffered for days, and Nancy did all she could do to help him but to no avail. Even though she sent word to Moses about his father, he never came to help. John knew he was dying and had his wife bring paper so he could write his will. In it he left everything to Nancy and Laura. Little Laura cried for days watching her dad suffer and eventually die on May 4, 1872.

Distraught and confused, Nancy took John's body back to Boles and buried him beside his first wife in Buffalo Cemetery. Little Laura cried all the way back and for several days after. Folks would say, "Don't cry; the little heiress should not cry her eyes out." Thus she was dubbed, "The Crying Heiress of Hot Springs" by Eliza Turman. Because Nancy was afraid to leave the will lying around, she carried it in her bosom pocket at all times.

After his burial Nancy took Laura and traveled back to Hot Springs. When they arrived they found everything they had had been destroyed. Because Mrs. Hobbs was hateful and threatened to kill the two of them, Nancy was terrified and asked for Moses' advice. He told her he thought it would be better for them to move back to Waldron and let the Hobbses take over the business (he, of course, stayed in Hot Springs with his wife).

When Nancy traveled to Waldron and reported what had happened to her husband, Mrs. Hobbs was arrested and convicted for Grandpa's murder. Even though she was put in the penitentiary at Little Rock, she still had control over the family's business affairs. Of course, it was through her husband that she continued to run things. Since she claimed to be a witch and have powers over people, many were superstitious and intimidated by her, so they did as they were told.

The "witch woman" had two clay dolls with nails sticking in them. The dolls represented a man and a woman. Ironically, she set them on top of a Bible. Whenever she wanted anyone to do her bidding, she would threaten them with the dolls, as if she could cause harm to them if they refused her demands. Of course, I never believed in witches, but many in those days did. Nancy was also terrified of her, especially after all that had transpired.

Although Nancy had the help of some really nice neighbors, William and Eliza Turman, who took them in, she raised Laura without a father. The Turmans had a pristine farmhouse about a mile from Waldron. They grew beautiful flower gardens and raised luscious grape vines and housed many beehives so they could produce honey. "Aunt" Eliza helped take care of Laura and made sure she was able to go to school.

Several years later Moses came to visit Nancy and advised her to ride back to Hot Springs and get the papers fixed legally, but she did not have a wagon in which to travel. When another man convinced her to put the papers on file in the courthouse at Waldron instead, she did so. That very night the courthouse burned to the ground. Laura was 12 years old by then and watched as it finished burning.

The only other record they had of the property was in Nancy's blue Bible. It was very common in those days for people to keep records of important events in the family Bible. I remember seeing it and reading "half interest in Hot Wells 440 Square lots" and something about "a township of land."

Even though my grandmother knew the property belonged to her and Laura, she realized the official will had been destroyed; so she felt helpless that she couldn't do anything about it. She worked with the sick and delivered many babies as a way to earn a living. In fact she gained such a great reputation, it was reported that people would rather call on her than the local doctor, Donovan, when they had problems or when the ladies of the community were in labor. Folks called her "Aunt Nancy."

"Aunt" Nancy Luella Pierce Blackwell
Circa 1875

Laura Blackwell
"The Crying Heiress of Hot Springs"
Circa 1880

2

In 1891-1892 something happened that changed my life, and my side of it should be told. The other side of the story has been told many times. I have heard it myself, and most of it is untruthful. I have heard both sides of this unbelievable, fantastic, distorted thing they call "fate," but it was a plan by the master mind of Satan himself and merely carried out by his agents. It worked so well, it is a shock to know the truth of it.

I could not bear this thing were it not for God's help and His own son Jesus, my Lord and Savior, who died on the cross to redeem me. His great love has sustained me in my darkest hour of despair. He has lifted me up as His own. For He is a father to the fatherless. Even a mother like mine can forsake her child, yet God has not forsaken me.

Thomas "Tom" Hamer Williams was born in Ohio in October of 1860. He was 20 years-old and had brown hair and striking blue eyes when he left Ohio after his dear mother had passed away and his dad had remarried. Since his father had a good friend, William Turman, down near Waldron, Arkansas, he decided to make a fresh start there. When he met 15 year-old Laura, he fell in love with her and asked for her hand in marriage. Flattered at the thought of becoming independent, she accepted his proposal. The two were married at the Turman residence.

The young couple bought and paid for 40 acres of land with a farmhouse from Mr. Tom Bates about a mile from Waldron, Arkansas. My father tended beautiful gardens and raised healthy livestock. Anyone who knew him understood he possessed a meek and gentle spirit, even to the lowly beasts of the fields. He had such a tender heart for animals that he would always admonish anyone who bought a horse or mule from him to *never* abuse it.

Because there was no railroad in town, he also earned money by hauling freight for the local grocers, farmers, and merchants to Fort Smith (50 miles to the north) and back to Waldron. His reputation for honesty brought him many satisfied customers. Although they had a hard life, Tom was content with the large family he and Laura had created, and he worked extremely hard to make everyone happy.

Joe Thomas owned the farm next to ours and had a couple of boys a little older than my brothers. There was a thin tree line that separated our place from theirs, but their boys and pigs had worn a trail through it. Other than the children occasionally interacting, the adults rarely saw one another.

On the opposite side, Charlie and Mattie Jones and their family owned a large farm. In fact they had more land than they were working, so my dad purchased an additional 40 acres from them. Pa made the down-payment with a mule and planned to pay off the balance from his freight business proceeds. Because Charlie (also known as "Ceo") and Mattie owned the Waldron Milling Company in town, they provided many loads of freight for my father's freight business. Basically, they were just great neighbors in every way possible.

Across the road and catty-corner to our farm were some other wonderful neighbors, Fletch and Mollie Jenkins. Mollie was always quick to help us any time there was a need. From what I was told she had helped whenever there was an illness or accident and had assisted my mother and grandmother after my siblings and I were born. She was always a kind soul. With the beautiful hills and farmlands and neighbors nearby, it appeared to be an ideal setting for any family to be raised.

It was a frigid 26th day of January in 1891 that I was born. My grandmother, Nancy Blackwell, lived with us and even delivered me. That was one of many reasons I have always felt a close connection to her. Hers was the first face I beheld in this harsh, cruel world, and her hands were the first ones to touch mine; she was also the first one to swaddle me close and kiss my face. My crib was even set in her bedroom next to her bed which had tall night posts on the corners. (I still have an image of her wearing a lace night cap when she retired for the night.)

I was the youngest of five children. My two brothers, George and Dock, were eight and six, respectively. Dock turned seven the following month. Emma and Nancy, my two sisters, were four and three at the time. Because Nancy was named after my grandmother, and her name was shortened to Nan later on, I will use the latter one so I do not confuse you as to which Nancy I am referring to.

My grandmother was tending to my mother after delivering me.

"Mama, I need some cool water from the well," Laura requested.

"Sure." Nancy, who was holding the swaddled infant, opened the bedroom door and yelled, "George, run get your ma a dipper of water, please."

"Yes'm." George ran out the front door to the well.

Tom, who had been pacing the floor in concern, coupled with anticipation, quickly made his way to the door. "How are they?"

Nancy smiled. "Come on in, Tom. They are both fine. You have another precious daughter, and she appears to be a strong, healthy one."

Tom, a little unsure of himself, took the baby and kissed her little forehead. Tears welled in his eyes. "She's beautiful, Laura!"

His wife smiled and nodded in agreement.

"Yes, she is a doll, just like the rest of them," interjected Nancy. "There's nothing to make a grandmother more proud than to help bring her little ones into this world. Anyone who doesn't believe in a supreme creator hasn't experienced the miracles that I have all these years."

"I know exactly what you mean," Tom responded. "Our children are truly miracles and blessings from the good Lord. I'd argue with anyone who said otherwise."

George returned with the dipper, slowly opened the door, and handed it to his grandmother. His eyes widened when he saw the baby.

"Thank you, Honey." Nancy made her way to the bed and helped lift Laura's head.

"Thanks, Mama." Laura took several sips of the cold liquid and handed back the dipper.

Seeing the look on his son's face, Tom leaned down with his new daughter. "This is your new sister, Ida. Do you want to hold her?"

"Sure!"

"Then sit down in that chair" -- he pointed -- "and I'll let you hold her."

Quickly, the boy sat down and looked eagerly as his father handed him the little one. He leaned down and kissed the baby. "Ida, I'm your big brother, George. I'm going to help take care of you, I promise." Smiling, he rocked his new sibling and tenderly palmed her little face.

As he took the infant back, Tom suggested, "Okay, why don't you run tell the others to come in and see their new sister."

"Yes, sir." George dashed out the door in excitement.

Shortly, the others returned and looked awestruck at Ida. The three of them began rubbing her little arms and kissing her. Since they all wanted to hold her, Tom and Nancy helped while each child took his or her turn.

"She's so pretty!" announced Emma. She rubbed Ida's arms.

"Yes, she is," agreed Nan, leaning down to kiss her.

Dock, a little hesitant, smiled and rubbed her face.

Tom took Ida and handed her back to Laura while Nancy finished cleaning the room. "Okay, it's time for you kids to let your mom rest now; she's had a hard day. I've got to get out back and tend to the stock, myself."

The whole house was humming with excitement but also with a lot of work due to the little newcomer. George and Dock went about their chores of bringing in firewood and stoking the fire while Emma and Nan ran small errands for Laura and Nancy. Because they were still quite young, their chores were limited to retrieving diapers or other items when requested; however, they were full of enthusiasm at doing so.

The next week, during Tom's lunch break, he came home to a busy Nancy preparing lunch.

"Tom, do you think Laura and the baby will be up to going to church next Sunday?"

"I reckon so. By then Ida will be nearly two weeks old."

"Good! I am so anxious to show this little one off to everyone. The ladies will be in such a tizzy," she chuckled. "It gives me great pleasure just watching everyone carry on when a new baby comes through the door. It's like a dose of medicine for the soul."

Tom grinned. "I'm sure it is. I'll go get Laura so we can eat."

Turning toward Emma and Nan who were playing in the living room floor, he said, "Emma, run get George and Dock to come in and eat."

"Okay!" Emma darted out the front door with Nan following her. When the four children returned, the adults had already made their way to the table. Nancy was setting the food in place.

"Where's Ida?" George wanted to know.

"She's sleeping in her crib like a little angel," his father replied. Turning toward his wife, he spoke. "Laura, honey, do you think you'll be up to going to church next Sunday?"

Laura hesitated. "I don't know. Maybe."

"Your mom's anxious to show off the baby," he chuckled.

"We'll see."

Nancy, a little concerned, looked at her daughter. "Are you not feeling well, Hon?"

"I'm okay, just a little tired."

"I'll have to mix you up a tonic that will help put some spring back in your step."

"Your mom's right, Laura. A good tonic wouldn't hurt you one bit. You've been through a lot."

The truth was Laura had not been cheery for quite a while, but the family was not sure why. Nancy and Tom both had tried doing things to lighten her load; however, there seemed to be something brewing under the surface. They just could not figure it out.

One day Nancy pulled Tom aside and suggested, "Maybe it's the baby blues."

"If we get her out of the house a little, maybe she'll perk back up," Tom replied.

The following Sunday, the family busied themselves in order to make the mile journey to church on their wagon. Salem was the children's favorite horse, and he was one of the two horses used to pull them along.

"Pa, please don't ever sell Salem," Emma requested.

"Don't worry, Honey, I wouldn't do that to you kids because I know just how much you love him. I'll keep ole Salem around here forever." He winked at her. "Besides, I love Salem as much as you do."

"Good!" Emma smiled. The children were all pleased.

Upon arrival the ladies buzzed around the little one like bumblebees around a daisy, one taking the infant and making such a fuss until another would take her and pass her around like a new doll. There was new life in the little congregation. Hymnal singing was exceptional that morning.

Finally, life returned to normal around the farmhouse and winter morphed into spring. Even though the brothers loved their family, they were typical boys for their ages -- always running around barefoot and getting into mischief whenever they had an opportunity. It was a way to entertain themselves and make life more enjoyable in the face of all the hard work that they all had to do around the place.

One day they discovered their dad leaning under the shade of a large oak with his hat pulled down over his eyes, napping. Emma and Nan were not far away inside the chicken coop gathering eggs when George and Dock, obviously up to one of their pranks, came inside the pen, snickering. Curious, the girls watched as George picked up a stick and scooped up a small amount of chicken droppings on the end of it, then picked up a feather and handed it to Dock.

Stealthily, they made their way to the back of the large oak. George reached around and placed the excrement on his father's index finger. Then Dock took the feather and tickled his nose. When the young man reached up and rubbed his nose and realized what had happened, he yelled, "Crap!" The boys burst into laughter and shot off like a bullet. Thankfully for the boys, their dad had a sense of humor because he was a prankster himself at a young age. He just shook his head and chuckled.

"Boys!"

He found the boys hiding inside the barn. "Since you boys seem to need something to do, I want you to go pull weeds from the garden."

"Yes, sir," the boys both answered in unison and took off giggling.

That evening when the family gathered around the table for supper, Tom told Laura that he was going to have to make another delivery to Fort Smith for some local businessmen. These trips usually took several days, depending on the weather. He would make his mile trek into town, load supplies from different farmers and merchants, and deliver them to businessmen in Fort Smith. After spending the night there, he would load things that were to be brought back to Waldron for businessmen and people in town. Tom earned a good living for the family because he wanted what was best for them, but it was hard for all of them whenever he had to be away.

Early the next morning, Tom, with the help of his two sons, loaded the wagon and prepared the horses that would pull the load for him.

"Pa, can I please go with you?" George pleaded.

Tom tenderly touched his son's head. "Son, I really need you to be the man of the house while I'm away. There's a lot you can do around here to help out your mother and grandmother."

George scowled.

"I tell you what…when Dock gets a little older and can take your job as the man around here, I'll let you go with me. How does that sound?"

The youngster smiled. "Yes, sir!"

Turning to his brother, he said, "Did you hear that, Dock? You will get to be the head of the house while Pa and I are away. You just need to hurry up and grow some more."

Tom chuckled.

Nancy, who was carrying Ida, came out the back door. Emma and Nan ran around her toward their dad. Laura took her time in following from behind. She seemed distracted somehow, periodically looking toward the tree line next to the farm, then to her husband. Emma and Nan grabbed their dad and hugged him. Tom leaned down and picked up each girl and kissed both in turn. "You girls be good for your ma while I'm away. Okay?"

"Yes, sir," each replied.

Nancy made her way with the baby. Tom took Ida and gave her a kiss. "I sure am going to miss her." He smiled at his mother-in-law. "Is there anything I can bring back for you, Nancy?"

"You might bring some sorghum syrup. I think we're about out, and you know them biscuits aren't the same without it." She smiled at him.

"You're absolutely right. Those delicious biscuits of yours are even better with syrup." He winked. Looking toward the baby, he said, "Don't grow too much while I'm gone, Honey. Pa will be back as quick as I can." He handed back the baby as he saw his wife approaching.

Walking toward her, he put his arm around her shoulder and gave her a squeeze. "Laura, is there anything I can bring you? I know you haven't seemed yourself lately."

"Maybe a string of glass beads and some toilet water."

"Is that all? If that is what will make you happy, I'll be glad to bring you some glass beads and toilet water, Honey."

"Yeah, that'll do for now." Laura stole a glance at the tree line again.

"Laura, is there anything wrong?"

She fidgeted a little. "No, there's nothing wrong," but her body language said otherwise. She pulled away from him. "I'll be fine."

Tom looked toward Nancy, who was watching, and shrugged. "Well, guess I'd better get on the road then." He climbed onto the wagon and motioned for the horses to go, all the while watching his wife. It had not seemed to matter what he had said or done for her lately, he just could not figure out what was really going on inside her mind. *I know it's been a few months since Ida was born, but it will probably just take longer this time for her to fully recover.* That was the only thought that made sense to him.

After Tom had disappeared from sight, the children ran off to play in the cornfield while the women went back inside with the baby. George caught Dock and shoved him down. They rolled in the dirt, laughing.

Emma shook her head in disgust. "Boys..."

Nan smiled.

The girls loved the entertainment their brothers provided them. They were always a comfort to the younger ones, especially when their dad was away on his business trips.

The sudden appearance of a man from the tree line next to them made them freeze. He was making his way to their back door. Dock was curious.

"Wonder who that is."

"Don't know, but I think he's the one I saw over at Mr. Thomas' the other day when I took one of their pigs back that got loose," George responded.

"Wonder what he wants."

"No telling."

Cautiously, Emma and Nan stepped closer to their brothers. They all watched with curiosity as their mother emerged from the house, whispered something into the man's ear, and walked off with him toward Joe Thomas' place. The girls ran after their mother.

"Where ya going, Ma?" Emma inquired.

Laura stopped and turned around. "Girls, this is Charlie Thomas. His uncle is Mr. Joe, the one that owns the farm next door. He wants to show me something over there. You kids stay here," she demanded.

"Yes, ma'am."

They watched as the two disappeared into the tree line that separated the two farms. Disappointed, the girls returned to their brothers and relayed the information.

"I don't think Pa would like it one bit," George snarled.

The others looked concerned. Emma wanted an explanation.

"Why not?"

"Because...Just 'cause." His tone told her he was in no mood to explain.

The girls decided to run back inside and talk to their grandmother about the issue. Maybe she could shed a little more light on things. The boys remained outside to keep an eye on the place while their mother was away. Besides, they were a little anxious about her leaving like she did. George remembered what his dad had said about him being the man of the place while he was away, and he was determined to do just that.

A couple of hours passed before Laura made her way back through the pig trail to their farm. Spotting his mother, George nudged Dock. "She's back."

They ran toward her.

"Why did you go to Mr. Thomas' place?" Dock inquired.

He had never seen his mother go to the Thomas farm for a visit before. The boys had been the only ones there, and that was on rare occasions to play with Joe's boys. More times than not, the Thomas boys would show up on the Williams' place.

"Charlie just wanted to show me something, that's all."

"What did he show you?" George asked.

Laura hesitated in thought. "Oh, he was just showing me some of his uncle's garden. It's really a nice one, and he has lots of peas this year."

What's so great about a bunch of peas? George wondered. He was not convinced. Besides, they had plenty of peas themselves. When she saw her son glaring at her, she turned and went toward the house.

Turning back, she yelled, "You boys clean up before supper."

"Yes, ma'am," Dock responded.

That evening the boys were up to one of their pranks again. George went into the girls' room and tied a piece of twine to the end of Emma and Nan's quilt by looping it through one of the stitches on top. Snickering, he motioned for Dock to take the ball of twine and head toward their room. George made sure he forced the string along the wall inside the chair legs so as not to be conspicuous.

After supper that evening and after all their chores had been finished, the boys were anxious for the girls to crawl in bed and get under their cover. It was then that they pounced. As the cover began creeping off the bed, the startled girls jumped up.

"What is that?" Nan gasped.

Emma saw the string attached to the quilt and followed it into the hall where she saw George and Dock bolt toward their room, laughing.

"It's the boys again!" She untied the twine from the quilt. Exasperated, Emma and Nan found the boys in their room under their covers, giggling. "You boys stop it and go to sleep!" But despite all that, Emma couldn't help but grin. Relieved, Nan realized it was all in fun and smiled. They returned to their room for the night.

The next afternoon while the boys were cleaning the barn and hauling out the manure to the garden, they saw Charlie Thomas coming from the pig trail again. Perturbed, George threw down the pitch fork. "I don't understand why he's back over here again. If he's got business here, he needs to wait and talk to Pa when he gets home."

"Why?" Dock did not quite understand.

"I just don't like it, that's why."

They watched as their mother exited the house, took Charlie's hand, and the two made their way toward the tree line again. When she spotted the boys, she yanked her hand from Charlie's. "You boys finish cleaning the barn and go help your grandmother when you're done. I'll be back in a little while."

"Where you goin', Ma?" George expected an explanation.

"We've got some business over at the Thomas place." George's skepticism made Laura uncomfortable. "Mind your manners and do as I say." The two started off, and Charlie nodded toward the boys.

"I can't wait until Pa gets back," George snapped.

"Me, too," Dock agreed.

George took up the issue with his grandmother. "Why is Ma running over to the Thomas place all of a sudden?"

Nancy studied the child for a moment. "Do you remember us talking about someone cheating me and your mother out of our property at Hot Springs years ago?"

"I think so."

"Well, Mr. Thomas told your mother that he is going to try and help get our property back."

"But Pa is the one who tends to all the business around here."

"I know. I'll be glad when he gets home."

"Me, too."

"I wouldn't say anything to your pa about it just yet."

"Why not?"

"We don't want to worry him any. He has a lot on his mind right now. He doesn't need anything else to concern him."

George agreed with her. *Maybe that's part of being the man of the house while Pa is away.* At least that thought pacified him for the moment.

The rest of the week was spent with everyone doing their chores around the little farmhouse. Nancy and Laura took care of Ida. While the women were busy cleaning and cooking, the children went outside and played; however, before they could, they had to take care of the animals first. Between feeding them and gathering the eggs from the chicken coop, this took a good portion of their days. But children will be children, and there was always time for fun. It seemed, however, their fun was interrupted on most days while their father was away by the sudden appearance of the man from next door.

Finally one afternoon while the children were playing, Nan spied her father riding up on his wagon. "Look! Pa's home!" They all ran toward him and waited for him to stop the horses and climb down from the wagon.

Tom reached out and hugged each child in turn. "I sure am glad to be home! Seeing all of you waiting to see me makes all those long, hard trips worthwhile." Looking around the place, he was pleased to see things in order. "Looks like you kids have been helping around here."

"Yes, sir, we have," Dock responded. George nodded in agreement.

"Nan and I have, too." Emma wanted to make sure her father understood the girls' efforts as well.

"Well, you all have done a mighty fine job, and I have a surprise for you."

He reached around to the back of the wagon and pulled out a sack of stick candy. One-by-one he handed the children their reward.

"Thank you, Pa" was the response from each.

"You are welcome. I wouldn't think of not bringing you children a treat when I have to be away for so long."

Tom had the horses pull the wagon inside the barn, then unfastened them before unloading the women's items and heading toward the house.

"George, when you and Dock finish your candy, would you feed and water the horses for your tired and sore ole' Pa?"

"Sure! We'll be glad to, Pa."

"Yes, sir," Dock replied. The truth was the children all missed the two horses when they were away, especially Salem. Salem had always been gentle with them and seemed to respond well when they rode him. All seemed to be at peace in their little neck of the woods when their father was home.

Thomas "Tom" Williams
Circa 1880

3

Summer found the family busy as usual. Although most of the crops had already been harvested and canned for the coming winter, livestock still had to be fed and watered, and the barn still had to be kept clean. George and Dock usually loaded the manure onto a wagon, then hauled it to the garden area so the field would be fertilized for the following spring. Sometimes the girls liked to follow them to the barn and help when they could. It made them feel important, but they mostly enjoyed the company of their older brothers. The boys were always up to something, and they sure did not want to miss any of it. Besides playing with Ida, the boys were their main source of entertainment.

Even though Laura helped her mother take care of the baby and worked around the house once in a while, it seemed most of those duties were left for Nancy. Laura seemed to take advantage of the fact that her mother was always working anyway, so she would disappear for a couple of hours now and then to visit some of the neighbors.

Ida was getting around on the floor by
scooting and crawling, so Nancy kept a close watch
on her. If she was busy in the kitchen, however, she
would have Emma and Nan watch her and play with
her. The girls loved that chore most of all. It was like
playing with a live doll, only their little doll was
getting much bigger and stronger by the day. If they
were sitting in the floor with her, Ida would crawl up
onto their laps. The girls would laugh at her and use
baby-talk to their little sister. Changing her wet
diapers was even fun for the two girls because they
loved her so much. Thankfully, they had never been
asked to change a dirty one. Their grandmother
usually volunteered for that job.

When Tom was home from his runs, he and
Nancy would usually load the family onto the wagon
on Sunday mornings to go to church. Most of the
time Laura would go with them, but occasionally she
would not feel up to it and would remain at the farm.
In her mind it gave her that needed respite from
family obligations and she could do as she well
pleased.

One Sunday morning when they were all
getting ready to leave for services, George and Dock
were already outside waiting on the others. Looking
around, George spied Dock grabbing a lizard and
putting it to his ear. "What do you think you're
doing?"

The lizard bit down on the boy's ear, and Dock let it dangle like an earring. "Thought I'd wear an ear bob this morning. The ladies do it all the time." The two laughed. About that time they heard the door slam. Dock yanked the lizard from his ear and stuffed it into his pocket.

"Better make sure Grandma and Ma don't see it."

"I will." Trying to be inconspicuous, they began petting Salem and his teammate and talking to them while the others made their way to the wagon.

Tom, who was holding Ida, waited while the others loaded onto the wagon, then handed the baby up to his mother-in-law, then climbed aboard next to his wife. While the seemingly happy clan wound its way around the curve and rode the mile to the little church building in Waldron, the girls began singing. Nancy would usually join in, and Ida would always get excited and start babbling. It had become a tradition for them, and they always looked forward to those rides into town to see some of their friends. Besides, it helped pass the time on those long trips. At least the trips seemed long to Emma and Nan.

Nancy glanced toward her grandson. "Dock, why is your ear bleeding?"

Sheepishly, the boys grinned. "Oh, guess I scratched it."

Sensing a problem with his wife, Tom tried to clear the air. "Laura, is there anything I can do to make things better for you?"

"No, I told you I'm fine."

He was not convinced. "Tom Bates might be willing to take the load to Fort Smith this week for me if his wife doesn't mind."

"No, don't be silly. We need the money too much."

"Are you sure, Laura?"

"I'm positive." Every time Tom had offered a solution to the obvious problem between the two, it was met with an instant refusal by her. He had worked so hard to make his wife happy by providing all of the family's needs. When he was home, he always made a special effort to spend time with the children and help lighten the load for the women. His own mother-in-law even seemed to be impressed with his efforts. *What else can I do?* were his only thoughts. He just could not figure it out.

When they arrived the boys jumped over the sides and helped the girls down while Tom tied the horses and helped Laura as she climbed down. Nancy handed the baby to her daughter and then made her way down. The children ran ahead and up the steps and inside the one-room building. During the week, the little church was transformed into a school house, but on the Lord's Day it was sacred to the townspeople.

After the usual greetings and hugs from different neighbors and friends, the Williams family made their way to one of the pews near the back. The adults sat nearest the center aisle. Next to them the girls took their place so they could help with their little sister. George and Dock liked to sit on the far end as far from their parents as possible. Their goal was to always pass that long hour of sitting by entertaining themselves.

As the congregation began singing its first hymn, Dock pulled the lizard from his pocket and put it to his ear once again, but the reptile did not bite down like the boy had anticipated. Instead it took off running across George's and the girls' laps, causing quite a commotion before it jumped down to the floor and ran toward the front of the building.

Their grandmother and their parents whirled toward them but did not see the lizard before it disappeared. Other members began squirming as it ran under their feet. One little girl squealed out. George and Dock giggled but were wary of their parents' attention. Finally, a gentleman up front halted its progress, picked the reptile up, and threw it out the side door. Once again the congregation returned to their singing.

When the minister dismissed the service, everyone began mingling. Because it was customary for the adults to visit for about half an hour before they were ready to go their separate ways, the children bolted for the doors. The half hour play time with their friends was what they looked forward to every time they were able to attend services. Sometimes the weather would hinder their attendance, and other times pure circumstances got in the way. Every opportunity to do so was relished.

Inside the women were visiting and passing around Ida and talking about their children and some of their shenanigans. "Can you believe those Thomas boys? They snuck over during the night and turned the Jones' outhouse over. At least that's what Mattie told me. It's just shameful what those boys get themselves into!"

Nancy wanted to make sure the others kept an eye out for the little delinquents.

"Now, Mom, they don't know it was them for sure."

"Well, they saw them running away and found their tracks the next morning that led straight to their farm."

"I saw those two out on the road late that evening." Mollie Jenkins was quick to aid Nancy. "They appeared to be up to something, and they were headed straight toward the Jones' place. They were carrying something, but I couldn't make out what it was."

"It certainly wouldn't be the first time those boys have gotten into mischief," Nancy pointed out.

The men had gathered near the front of the sanctuary sharing stories about their crop successes and failures and offering advice to one another. William Turman offered his expertise. "If you will plant your crops in different spots every year, they really do seem to do better."

His gardens were the envy of all, and he had many years of experience under his belt. He and his wife, Eliza, had helped many in the community by taking them into their home or providing food or financial help, and everyone listened to every word that came from either one's mouth. (In fact they were the same couple who had taken Nancy and Laura into their home decades earlier.) They were the epitome of what a true Christian was as far as their neighbors were concerned.

"I'll try that next spring," Tom responded. "Much obliged for the advice."

"Sure thing. I believe if you help your neighbor, you help yourself in more ways than one."

"That's a good way to look at it, Mr. Turman. Thanks again!"

Members eventually dispersed and went their separate ways. Most of them had ridden by horse and buggy, but the ones from town had walked because the weather was clear and dry. It only took about 15 minutes more for the little church house to once again claim its status as the little schoolhouse.

That afternoon Tom thought of another idea that might change Laura's indifferent attitude. Maybe she just needed a little fun in her routine. "Honey, why don't we load the kids up and go down to the lake and have a picnic? The kids can even go swimming."

The children were jubilant. Nancy even loved the idea, but Laura was not as enthusiastic as the others; however, she agreed to go. Nancy began making sure the children were dressed properly so they could go swimming, while Tom and Laura made the other preparations. An hour later Salem and his companion were once again pulling the Williams family down the road past Mollie Jenkin's house. When Nancy saw Mollie in her front yard and looking in their direction, the two women waved.

Arriving at the site of the small lake, the four older children were quick to jump down and sprint toward it. There was a tree with low-lying limbs which hung out over the water. Someone had already tied a long piece of rope that had been used to swing out over the lake and drop in. George was the first one to climb up and grab hold of it. Dock was right behind. Swinging out over the water, the eldest sibling yelled as he dropped.

"Splash!"

His audience cheered.

Ida was watching and laughing at the others. Nancy was guarding her closely. She stood the child up on her feet and helped her walk closer to the show. Ida would squeal once in a while as the children splashed into the lake. Since her grandmother was holding her hands, she would try to jump with excitement. It appeared the baby would soon be toddling around on her own.

Tom and Laura took a seat on a quilt they had spread over the grass. "Laura, I know I have to travel a lot, but you know I love you, don't you?"

"Yeah, I know you do." She looked toward the children. "Look at those kids. They sure are having fun." It was obvious she was trying to divert his attention. "Ida will be right in the middle of it all before you know it. She's already trying her best to do that. Why, if she sees the girls playing, she crawls right up to them. And when she sees George and Dock come in the house, she crawls straight to them and wants to be picked up. You can tell she adores her brothers."

Tom smiled. "Yeah, we sure have a great group of kids, Laura. I couldn't ask the good Lord for a better family. It's the main thing I miss when I'm away." Laura nodded. "You know I have to make those runs, don't you, Honey?"

"Yes, and I'm glad you do, Tom. It's the only way we can have all the things we have. I don't want you to stop hauling freight."

"Okay, I just thought that might be bothering you."

"No, it's not."

"Well, you know Mr. Turman and Mr. Bates need me to take another load for them up to Fort Smith this week, so I probably need to head out early in the morning."

"That'll be fine." She rose up and started toward the lake.

Tom followed but stopped to pick up Ida. He gave her a tight hug and kissed her cheek. *What I wouldn't give to feel that kind of hug from my wife again... How long has it been? It's hard to remember. Maybe when Ida doesn't need so much attention, Laura will feel differently.*

A rooster's crow woke the man at the first crack of dawn. Slowly, he made his way to the barn and began feeding the horses and preparing them for the harness. Nancy had heard him get up and had begun cooking breakfast for the family while the others still slept. One-by-one the family made their way to the kitchen and took their places around the table. Tom came in and joined them.

After they had made their greetings to one another, Tom interrupted with a concern. "Did any of you kids let a pig out of the pen? There's one missing."

They all shook their heads. "No, sir" was the response from the four older ones.

Ida spoke. "No."

Everyone laughed at her.

"Be sure to fasten any pens you open before you leave them. We don't want to lose any more animals. That pig would've grown into enough ham and bacon to last this family for a good while."

"Yes, sir," they responded.

Nancy's brows furrowed. "You don't think those Thomas boys could've taken it, do you?"

"Now, Mama, don't blame them," Laura blurted.

"What makes you say that, Nancy? Did you see something?" Tom knew his mother-in-law well enough to understand she did not make unwarranted accusations.

"I saw them at the tree line around back looking around, but they saw me and left. After the outhouse incident, I wondered what they were up to."

"Just keep an eye out. A prank is one thing. I don't know if they would go so far as to steal from their neighbors, though."

"I have a bad feeling about those two. I don't think the boys should play with them."

"Now, Mama, you know boys will be boys," Laura reminded her.

Nancy glanced toward Tom who shrugged. "Just the same, you kids keep an eye out and make sure you close any pens that might be open," he admonished them.

"We will," George responded. "I'll make sure of it while you're away."

"Thank you, son. You are a good man to have around the place while I'm away." Dock looked disappointed. "You, too, Dock. I appreciate both of you watching out for the women while I'm gone." Dock beamed.

As soon as breakfast was finished, Tom went out the back door with the family following behind. Giving the children their usual hugs and kissing Ida, he nodded toward Nancy then hugged Laura. "I'll try and bring you a surprise this time, Laura."

"Thanks. I appreciate it."

The patriarch of the small farm rode around the house to the road while everyone waved and shouted their goodbyes. He disappeared from view. Suddenly, his children felt lonely once again. Sure, they knew their grandmother was there to look after them even when their mother was away visiting neighbors, but they still missed their dad. How they wished he did not have to make those long journeys through the mountains as often as he did. The only solace was when they would see him riding up the road on his return trips. Those hugs and surprises he always brought back somehow made those absences bearable.

That afternoon Laura told her mother she had business to take care of concerning their property back in Hot Springs. "Charlie is going to try and help us get it back."

"I don't know how he is going to do that. Mrs. Hobbs has the run of the place, and possession is nine-tenths of the law. Besides, your dad's will was burned in the courthouse fire."

"Well, he is friends with Mr. and Mrs. Hobbs. They made a deal with him, and he plans to help us as much as he can. He swears if we do as he tells us, we'll get it back."

"I hope he knows what he's talking about, that's all."

"I'm sure he does, Mama. I'll be gone for a while today, but I'll let you know what I find out."

Nancy was doubtful, but she was hoping her daughter was correct. *We'll see*, she thought.

Laura stepped carefully through the pig trail and around to the Thomas farm where she saw Charlie sitting under a shade tree drinking some whiskey. When he noticed her, he jumped up and met her and gave her a hug. "Hey there, Laura. How's my lady this fine afternoon?" He offered her a sip.

"No, thanks. I just wanted to know if you've heard anything else about my mother's property."

"It's yours, too."

"I know, but Mama has the record written in her blue Bible that shows the property description and the date she and my father bought it. Remember, the will with my name on it was burned in the courthouse fire."

"Well, I'm still working on it, Laura. You just need to trust me; we'll get it back. Just wait and see." He thought a minute. "Why don't we go for a ride and get away where we can talk privately?"

"Sure."

Charlie untied his horse, climbed on, and then grabbed Laura's hand as she climbed up and sat behind him, wrapping her arms about his waist. With his flask of whiskey in hand, he managed to direct the horse away from the farm about a half mile to a familiar spot of theirs.

Laura climbed down and made her way to a shaded grove. Charlie followed her. Grabbing her close, he began kissing her passionately. The lovers took advantage of the privacy and spent the rest of the afternoon there. *What is it about Charlie that intrigues me so? He's the forbidden fruit, and I am Eve,* she decided.

That evening she explained to her mother how it would take some time, but Charlie was going to play his hand carefully to ensure they were able to get at least partial control of their property back.

"I guess I'll believe it when I see it done," was her response. "If ever there was anyone crazy in this old world, that Hobbs family is. I just don't see how Mr. Thomas is going to change that."

Tom Williams holding Nan (one-year)
George (6), Emma (2), and Dock (4)
1889

4

By the time September rolled around, George and Dock had celebrated birthdays, so they were a year older. Although George was in fourth-grade and Dock was in the second, all of the students shared the same classroom. Since Emma was not quite old enough to attend, she remained home with her two sisters but looked forward to attending with her brothers the following year. Tom had a fair education under his belt, but he was determined to see that his children had a good one. As long as the responsible old grandmother lived in the Williams' house, she also made sure the children attended school when he was away if it were possible because she understood how hard life would be for them without the proper schooling.

It had been a couple of weeks since Tom had hauled any freight, but he had a large order that had to be delivered the week school resumed session. The children had said their goodbyes and had promised their dad to help around the place as they always had. George and Dock were proud of the fact that their dad was an important businessman in the community because he worked with some of their classmates' parents; consequently, they felt important at school.

The boys had grown accustomed to their mother's frequent visits to the Thomas farm. Even though they did not approve, they usually were busy with chores or with finding things to entertain themselves and their sisters when they were home from school. The girls had also grown accustomed to their grandmother taking care of them, so they rarely questioned where their mother was if she were gone. It was just part of their life as they knew it.

It was obvious Nancy was not supportive of her daughter's comings and goings so much, but she vowed not to cause one ounce of trouble between the married couple. Tom was the best thing that had ever happened to Laura as far as she was concerned, and she hoped her daughter would come to her senses. She prayed for them daily.

Plans were being made for a fall festival at the little school house, and the children were all excited. The young teacher was bubbling with energy because she, too, enjoyed the holidays and mingled activities for it with their lessons of the day. They studied the fall season and the different plants and vegetables associated with that time of year.

Students drew and colored pumpkins and "Indian" corn to cut out and decorate the drab little classroom for the event. It did not matter if the classroom would transform into the Lord's house on Sunday. They figured the Lord would be well-pleased with their crafts, anyway. After all, he was the one who had bestowed them with such talents. They were content with their work. Sunday could not come quickly enough for them. It would be a chance to show off their efforts to their parents and to the community.

One day after Tom had left on another delivery to Fort Smith and the boys were away at school, Laura slipped off again to the Thomas farm to see Charlie. She took advantage of her mother watching the children whenever she felt a need to get away from the daily drudgery of family life.

She and Charlie made their usual trek to the area they had frequented and spread out a quilt. With his whiskey in hand, Charlie pulled his lover down next to him and offered her a drink. She took one sip but winced. It was too strong for her. Since she had never seen Tom drink whiskey, she had the illusion it somehow made Charlie look tough and masculine and even sexy.

"Laura, have you thought about my proposal?"

"Yes, but I can't just up and leave my family, Charlie. What would I do about Mama and the kids? Besides, we have the farm and all. I can't just walk off and leave it all."

"You know I can take care of you, Laura. I'm tellin' you, we can get part of your property back. Mr. Hobbs already promised me."

"Mama doesn't think he will turn it over to us."

"Hell, Laura, I told you I'm friends with the man. Besides, I'm a pretty shrewd businessman. You just have to trust me on this." Taking her hand and looking into her eyes, he asked, "Don't you trust me, Laura?"

"Yes, I trust you Charlie, but I don't know about trusting old man Hobbs. That's what Mama calls him. And from what I hear, Mrs. Hobbs is a witch. She's put spells on people before, then things happened to them."

"Yes, she is and that's why I know she can help us. I rode the train over to the pen with Mr. Hobbs and visited with her, and they gave me their word if you would marry me that they would include us in the business. They need me to help run it, you see."

"Are you sure?"

"Hell, yeah, I'm sure!"

"Alright, let me think about it. I've got to work things out first. It isn't going to be easy."

"I know, Laura, but think about it. We could live like kings and queens once we get into the bathhouse business. You and the kids would have everything you could ever ask for."

"But what about Mama?"

"Hell, she could have her own place," he laughed. "I'm telling you, we can have housemaids to help out around the place if you want them. You won't have to lift your pretty little hands to do anything you don't want. I give you my word."

Laura nodded. "Alright, Charlie, just give me a little time, that's all." Charlie pressed himself against her and kissed her lips. The passion in the woman was aroused. Was it the crudeness in his language or the fact that he offered something she had never had? Whatever the attraction, she succumbed once again to his advances.

Near the end of the week after Tom made it home, the children were bubbling with excitement about the upcoming fall festival. George and Dock had talked about it to the girls so much, they were just as enthused. Emma and Nan vaguely remembered the one the year prior, but the memory was enough to cause an eruption of emotion, so they jigged around the house all day and twirled their little sister around. Even though Ida was toddling about the house and sensed the enthusiasm, she was too young to understand what it was all about, but she joined in with the dancing the best she could and burst into laughter with the rest of them.

"Pa, will you be home for it?" George wanted to make sure.

"Why, I wouldn't miss your festival for anything else," his father reassured. "Besides, I want to see all of the work you boys have been doing at school. It's important, you know."

"Yes, sir." Dock was the first to respond.

"Yes, sir, it is," George echoed.

The lower temperatures of the season heightened the overall moods of the household. Even the old grandmother seemed to have a better attitude with her chores after suffering through the grueling summer months in the hot kitchen. Autumn just seemed to make a hard life much easier. *Maybe it's God's way of saying, "Well done, thou good and faithful servant,"* Nancy thought. *Not only does he give us the harvest, but he gives us relief from the heat.* All seemed well in their little corner of the world.

As long as Tom was home, Laura would stop her visits to the Thomases' place. Although she tried to stay busy around the house and on the farm, she kept a watchful eye out just in case Charlie appeared at the tree line. She kept thinking of his proposal and wondered how they would make it work, but the prospect of a new and better life lured her.

Charlie drank to pass the time until Tom was gone again and out of his way. He could not get the idea about living like kings and queens out of his mind and hoped to solve his dilemma soon because he knew what Mr. and Mrs. Hobbs had promised him. *If I marry Laura they will make me a partner.*

Late October finally arrived and with it the long-anticipated fall festival. Scientists had recently discovered a way to predict weather several days in advance, and word was out that a nice cold front was on its way. This was exactly what everyone wanted. After all, what was a fall festival without cold weather? Something about the dry, crisp air contributed to everyone's exhilaration over the event.

All the neighbors attended: Charlie and Mattie Jones and their children; Fletch and Mollie Jenkins; Tom Bates; all of the Williams family, and even the Thomas boys, along with the rest of the townspeople who arrived to take advantage of the annual social celebration. With each family came a barrage of foods -- everything from meats and vegetables to cakes and pies. The well out back provided attendees with plenty of drink.

As the Williams family waited their turn at the table, they scanned the room looking at the children's work. Both of their sons took great pride in showing them the pumpkins and corn they had colored and cut out for display. They also read the stories they had penned. When their grandmother and parents congratulated them on such beautiful artistry, they beamed at them, proud of their accomplishments.

After everyone had eaten to their content, the children ran around the grounds to play. The Thomas boys motioned for George and Dock, and the curious brothers ran toward them. "You two wanna bet with us?" The eldest challenged.

"Bet what?" George asked.

"Bet something big's going to happen."

Dock wanted to know, too. "Like, what?"

"Bet you brats will find out when you find out." He cackled. Then the two ran off.

George glanced toward Dock. "Don't mind them. They don't even know what they're talking about."

His brother nodded.

"Let's get back to the others."

When George reached his father and explained what the Thomas boy had told him, Tom looked puzzled. "I wouldn't pay them any mind, Son. I'm sure they're just messing with you."

Laura held her breath. *Did Charlie say anything to them about our plans? I sure hope not.* "You boys don't need to pay any attention to them. Your pa's right. They were just messing with you. Besides, you know what your grandmother said about not playing with them."

Nancy could not believe the change in Laura's attitude. *Maybe she's finally seeing how those boys really act. Maybe she'll quit spending so much time over there.* Those thoughts gave her some comfort at least.

Charlie took advantage of the two weeks that Tom was home to ride over to Hot Springs, visit with Mr. Hobbs again, and update him on his plans with Laura. Hobbs was in the bathhouse overseeing things when he walked in. The two shook hands.

"Well, what's the news?"

"Laura wants to marry me, but it's taking longer than I had planned."

"The sooner you make it happen, the better off you'll be."

"I'm doing the best I can. I just wanted to make sure you and your wife haven't changed your minds."

"Hell no, we haven't changed our minds," Hobbs reassured. "You haven't changed yours, have you?"

"No, sir. I just wanted to make sure the plan was still on and let you know about the delay."

"Just keep me posted on everything."

"I will." Charlie shook Hobbs' hand and left.

The two weeks passed too quickly for Tom, his children, and even his mother-in-law before he had to leave on another run, but the time crept by for Laura and Charlie. As soon as Laura was convinced Tom was out of her way, she slipped through the tree line and over to the Thomas farm. Charlie had been keeping an eye out for Tom to leave, so he met her. In one hand he had a bottle of whiskey; with the other he pulled her close. "Laura, I can't wait until you leave that son-of-a-bitch. You know you would be much happier with me, don't you?"

Laura smiled. "Yes, you know I would, Charlie. It's just a lot harder to do than I thought it would be. That's all."

"Well, once the splinter gets pulled out, it's a big relief. Just do it and get it over with, and we can move on with our lives and live like kings and queens."

"I know things will be better. I just need a little more time. It's the holiday season, and I don't want to ruin it for the kids. At least let's wait until after Christmas and New Year's."

Charlie did not like Laura's delay, but what else could he do? He had to play his cards right and win her over with care. He certainly did not want to force her into changing her mind. "I don't know how Mr. and Mrs. Hobbs are going to react to that much of a delay, but I'll let them know. Maybe they won't mind since their business kind of slows this time of year."

Late that afternoon after Laura had returned home, Charlie again made his way through the tree line. This time he was carrying a small pot with something inside. Curious, the children who had been tending to the chickens and livestock watched as he set it down beside the house and climbed the steps to the back door.

Answering the door, Laura was puzzled as to why he was there. "If you can let me see your mother's blue Bible with the records written down, it will help me in getting your property back."

"All right." She turned toward her mother's bedroom.

Since Nancy overheard him, she objected and followed her daughter into her room. "Laura, I don't want my Bible leaving my sight."

"Don't worry, Mama. Charlie just needs to see it so he can help us get our property back from the Hobbses."

"I just don't think he can do that. We never could."

"It's worth a try, Mama."

Against her mother's wishes, she proceeded to the back door and showed the Bible to Charlie. When he finished reading the page with the property description and purchase date, he asked if he could take it with him. Laura told him that her mother did not want it to leave her sight.

"At least I know what it says and can relay that information to Mr. Hobbs." Charlie thanked her and said his goodbyes to Laura and her mother and left. Laura closed the door and disappeared inside. She was afraid of making their relationship blatantly obvious to her mother.

When Charlie returned to the side of the house where he had left the pot, he motioned for the children to come to him. Cautiously, they approached him as he picked up the little pot. They watched as he sprinkled something under the house then said an incantation that made no sense to them. "An old witch gave this to me. It's a curse against all of you except your mother. She said you will all die -- that is, except your mother, and she will become rich."

The children were frightened and confused and were relieved when they saw Mr. Thomas leave.

George tried to reassure the others. "Don't pay any mind to him. That man's crazy if there ever was one."

Still the others were not completely at ease, but they trusted their brother and went back to their chores. When they had finished, they began playing again which helped relieve their anxiety about the incident.

Life around the Williams farm returned to normal once again, but the colder weather caused a change in the usual activities. Firewood had to be chopped and gathered near the house. Tom would cut the trees and chop them into small enough pieces so George and Dock could load them onto a wagon and pull them to the house, then pile them into neat stacks. Consequently, the two boys were becoming stronger and loved showing off their muscles to their sisters. The girls loved squeezing their arms; even Ida occasionally joined in. They were so impressed they believed their brothers could protect them from anyone or anything. Having two strong brothers around when their pa was away gave them a sense of security.

With Thanksgiving came the tradition of having their fill of the niceties of the harvest. The women were busy in the kitchen preparing pies, roasting turkey and sweet potatoes, and basting venison. These were all done inside the wood-burning stove that helped warm the house. Aromas permeated throughout the home and gave the family great satisfaction and created much anticipation.

Once the Williamses had written another
holiday into its book, Tom had a few weeks respite
from his freight deliveries. He thoroughly enjoyed
playing games with the children. If the weather
hindered their outdoor activities, they would play
hide-n-seek inside. One of the girls' favorite places to
hide was under their bed. However, Ida would crawl
under it with them and would babble and
occasionally say words. Emma and Nan would try to
quiet her when they heard their pa coming toward
them, but he never let on.

"I wonder where those girls went to."

No matter how quiet they tried to be, they
would usually snicker. It was a special time in their
young lives, and their devotion to their father was
steadfast. Every moment they spent with him was
relished.

Their brothers felt the same way toward him,
but their ideas about playing varied somewhat from
their sisters'. They loved rough-housing and playing
pranks the most. Tom would get them down on the
floor and wrestle with them. Because he knew the
world was a tough place to exist, he wanted his boys
to grow into fine, strong men. George and Dock were
always challenging him to an arm-wrestling contest.
Sometimes their pa would let them win but not
always. In his own way Tom was teaching them to
deal with success and failure. He had certainly had
enough of both.

Christmas was upon them before they had
fully savored Thanksgiving. Since it was the most
anticipated holiday of the year, the children helped in
cutting a tree and decorating it. It was the most
important adornment to their living room, and they
loved the suspense and anticipation of presents
suddenly appearing beneath it. All of the children
played guessing games as to what might show up
Christmas morning.

"It will be candy," Emma proposed.

"I think it will be fruit and nuts," Dock
speculated.

"I'm hoping for a knife," George suggested in
hopes of receiving one.

"I hope it's candy, too," Nan added.

"Candy!" Ida blurted. Everyone laughed at
her. She was quickly becoming a valuable part of the
Williams clan, and they all loved her dearly.

The best part of the holiday season was not the
food or the presents but the time they all spent
together. This was the time of year Tom vacationed
from his freight business, and everything seemed at
peace in the world. As far as the children were
concerned, the Williams family was gratified and
complete.

Nan, Ida, Emma
Circa 1893

5

Although most of the family thoroughly enjoyed the holiday season due to Tom being home more often, Laura was getting antsy. She had not been able to make her rendezvous with Charlie Thomas for a few weeks. One day she saw him peeking from the tree line, so she slipped him a note she had been carrying in her apron pocket for just such an occasion by leaving it on a stump and turning for the house. When she reached the back porch, she turned to make sure he picked it up. The last thing she wanted to happen was for someone else to find it. After he read the message, he waved at her and disappeared.

That afternoon a telegram in town warned residents of an impending snow storm – which was very likely to turn into a blizzard -- due to hit the Waldron area in about a week, so Charlie made a flying trip to inform his partners in Hot Springs that conditions would be perfect for the event. Immediately, their plan was put into motion.

Although Tom knew nothing about the weather report, he made his preparations as quickly as he always did during winter months because he never knew what to expect. The faster he could move the better he and his horses would be in case the temperature plummeted and quickly became worse. After the usual hugs, kisses, and goodbyes, the dear father rode off.

The next week moved in and with it the leading edge of the cold front. Winds began to howl, and the snow began falling heavily. George and Dock were in charge of bringing in the firewood and keeping the fireplace aglow. Emma and Nan entertained Ida and helped the women inside the house. There was a little anticipation over Ida's upcoming first birthday, and the girls were making plans for it to be a special one.

Startled by a sudden knock, George slowly cracked the door open. Carrying a bottle of liquid in one hand, Charlie shoved the door open and entered. He brushed the snow off his sleeves and stomped his feet.

"Good day, ladies. I just wanted to warn you there's a bad storm coming in, and it's making a lot of people deathly sick."

"Really?" Laura gasped.

"No worries, though. I have some medicine that will stop you from catching it."

Worried, Laura asked more about it. "What is it, Charlie?"

"It's something like pneumonia, but this" – holding up the bottle of medicine – "is guaranteed to stop a person from catching it. I've already taken some to make sure I don't get it myself." When Laura tried to take the bottle from him, he stopped her. "You ladies just sit down and let me fix the right dose for you. I know how it's supposed to be mixed." He turned and disappeared into the kitchen.

With a dose for each, he returned to the living room and made sure which one he gave Nancy first. She shuddered. "That's the worst medicine I've ever tasted."

Then he handed Laura her dose, and she swallowed it. "It's not that bad, Mama."

"What about the children?" Nancy inquired.

Hesitant, he replied, "Oh, that sickness doesn't affect children, just the adults."

The women were puzzled.

"That's what a doctor told me. Don't worry about the kids."

It was at this moment when the mother and daughter had become unsuspecting participants in a devious plan spawned from the loins of Satan himself.

Nancy began moaning and clutching at her stomach. "I think that medicine *made* me sick. I'm going to go lay down." She managed to pick up Ida and take her to their room and placed her in the crib before she sprawled out on her own bed.

Laura became very groggy and could not stay awake. "Charlie, that medicine made me *so* sleepy."

"That medicine is *supposed* to make you sleepy so you can get some rest and not come down sick, Laura."

The children were extremely worried at the spectacle taking place in their own living room, so they disappeared into the girls' bedroom.

"When will Pa be home?" Dock wanted to know.

"I'm not sure, but Grandma said he would normally be coming in tonight if the weather doesn't slow him down," George answered. "But I'll sure be glad when he does."

The boys remained with the girls until they fell off to sleep, then went to their own room for the night. *What else can we do?* George asked himself. The young boy was accustomed to problem-solving, but never in his nine years had he faced this kind of dilemma. Before it had always been the women who had made the decisions when his father was away. He thought about his father's expectations of him being the man of the house while he was gone.

Eventually, Tom rode up to the farm and put his horses in the feedlot so they could eat. When he entered his house, Charlie and another man who had made his appearance at the Williamses' house met him and shook his hand.

"Good evening, Mr. Williams. I heard the women were down sick, so we brought them some medicine. There's a new sickness going around that has killed quite a few folks, so we brought something to keep them from catching it." Charlie showed him the bottle.

Tom had met Charlie before but had no suspicions about him; he only knew he was related to their neighbor next door. "Thank you, Mr. Thomas. Much obliged." He took off his coat and hung it nearby. "Are they alright?"

"They will be when the medicine takes effect. I'll mix the right dose for you like I did for the women."

While he was in the kitchen preparing his dosage, Nancy heard what was going on and made her way to the living room. She told Tom that she did not think it was a good idea to take the medicine because it seemed to have made her sick. The other man shook his head no.

Charlie reappeared. "I assure you, Mr. Williams, it wasn't the medicine that made her sick." Handing the glass to him, "Here, take this before you come down with what they have."

"Thanks." Shuddering, he swallowed the medicine, then washed it down with some water. It wasn't long before the liquid started causing Tom excruciating stomach pain and forcing him to double over. "Mr. Thomas, I believe I'll go on to bed; I'm not feeling well. That trip in this weather has gotten the best of me."

"You go right ahead, Mr. Williams. I will see that things are taken care of around here. I already put the children to bed."

The following day George sent the girls for help. He did not trust the two men in his house, and he had never taken care of sick adults before and was quite overwhelmed. The women had always been the ones to take care of them when they were ill. When the neighbors arrived at the Williams' house, Charlie and the other man told them that they were handling things but appreciated their concern. The Williams' friends left believing the adults probably had pneumonia.

Later that afternoon there was a lot of hammering going on next-door at the Thomas farm. Even though Nancy was in much pain, she managed to send Dock over to find out what they were building. One of the boys who had taunted them before replied sarcastically, "They are making coffins for your dad and grandma." Shocked, Dock rushed back home and reported this to his grandmother.

Although Nancy had never put much stock in anything the Thomas boys said, she was still concerned. *Why would they say such a mean thing to anyone? Those boys are awful!* "Don't pay any attention to those boys, Dock. I don't want you going over there anymore. You hear?"

"Yes,m." The seven year-old darted back to be with his siblings.

When he reported what the Thomas boy had said to him, George spouted, "Those boys are as crazy as a pile of bed bugs. Grandma is right; we need to stay away from them." That was just fine with the others because they had no intention of ever stepping foot on the place again. Between the man with the pot containing the "witch's curse" and his two younger cousins, evil seemed to radiate from that farm, and they wanted no part of it.

The next day Charlie opened the front door, stepped out onto the front porch and signaled some men over. Joe Thomas and another man came up and talked things over with him. They were laughing and drinking whiskey and gave Charlie a bottle. Then they made themselves at home in the living room.

The men became loud and obnoxious. To investigate, the children snuck toward the living room but tried to keep as hidden as possible. The drunken strangers in their house terrified them. Never before had they stumbled upon such a scene. George thought, *What are we to do?* They heard the moans of their dear father and went to his door. He had been resting in the boys' room so he did not disturb his wife. Laura was drugged and sound asleep, so she knew nothing about Tom being home. Often he had to jump and run to the outhouse due to the sudden onslaught of diarrhea.

Tom motioned for the boys to come in. George and Dock were quick to respond. The boys were startled to see their father in so much distress. He had always been the strong one in the family. Raising his head, Tom whispered. "I think those men are trying to kill me." To see him pale and in such noticeable pain and unable to deal with the intruders terrified them.

George's eyes widened. "How do you know, Pa?"

"They keep coming to the door and looking in here and laughing. I can tell by the look in their eyes, and I've never had my mouth and throat hurt like this before. I think your grandma was right about the medicine."

The children were terrified more than ever. The girls, who had been listening, retreated to their bedroom and burst into sobs. Their brothers followed them and began trying to devise a plan to help their father. George looked out the window and saw the snow falling in drifts. It was the most snow he had seen falling in his young life. He glanced around toward the front of the house and caught the sight of one of the men with a lantern who was backing a wagon toward the front porch. There was a casket in the back end.

The boys rushed back toward their father, but Charlie saw them. "You boys get your asses here!" he demanded, pointing to his side. They did as they were told. Then the four men seized Tom, who was too weak to fight them all, and carried him out.

Nancy, who was extremely sick herself, saw what was happening before her very eyes and yelled out from her room. "Tom, Tom, wake up!"

She thought he was sleeping, but the boys watched in horror as the men transported their moaning father out the front door and put him into the coffin, then nailed the lid shut. Nancy, who had also dealt with severe stomach pain and diarrhea, was too weak to follow.

"Please, mister!" George pleaded.

"Please, sir!" Dock begged, grabbing the man's leg.

Joe Thomas shoved him down. "Look! What your dad's got is contagious, and we have to bury him before anyone else catches it."

"But he ain't even dead!" George blurted."

Charlie Thomas roared, "Hell, he *will* be by the time we get him to the cemetery!"

His three coconspirators erupted in raucous laughter. He directed the other men to take the boys along so they didn't run off and alert any of the neighbors while they were gone.

"You boys get up there by your pa. You can have your last ride with him to the cemetery," Joe instructed them.

They climbed onto the wagon and sat next to the casket. All the way through the stormy night, they wept as they heard the moans and groans of their beloved father. By the time they made it to the Square Rock Cemetery, the four men were even more inebriated.

"Get down from there! You bastards better do as you're told, or you will be the next ones buried!" one of the men yelled to the boys.

The siblings jumped down from the wagon and got out of their way.

Charlie spouted off, "Boys, I'll be pulling the strings over your daddy's mules in less than three weeks!" Then he chuckled at himself.

George motioned for Dock to hide behind a tree. Shivering with cold, they huddled together and watched through the snowfall and lantern light as the drunken men buried their helpless dad and patriarch alive. George had an idea. "Let's get Charlie Jones to help us come back and dig Pa up when we get home." Dock agreed. That was the best idea either had at the moment.

By the time the four men and the two siblings had ridden back to the Williamses' home, the men passed out in the living room to sleep off their liquor. George and Dock slipped off to their grandmother's room to inform her about their plan. Ida was asleep in her crib. Nancy was ghastly pale and moaning. "Be careful, boys," she feebly whispered.

Grabbing their coats this time, the boys dashed out through the blinding snow toward Charlie and Mattie Jones's house where they banged furiously on the front door. "Mr. Jones!" they both yelled.

Mr. Jones threw open the door. "What is it?"

"Please, Mr. Jones, we need your help! Some men buried Pa alive, and we need you to come with us and help dig him up!"

Confused, Mr. Jones shook his head. "You boys must be mistaken. Nobody is going to bury anyone alive."

"But they did!" George insisted.

"Yes, sir, they did!" Dock added.

"No, I'm sorry about your pa, but I know he was really sick. Now you boys get on home before you catch your death."

"Please sir," George begged.

"I can't leave Mattie. She's really sick. Now you boys get on home like I told you, or you two will be sick. This is no kind of weather for you to be out in, especially these late hours." He closed the door.

Crying, the boys ran back to their house and reported the news to their sisters and grandmother. They went back outside and found a shovel. When they tried to see if it was sharp enough, they realized the ground was frozen like rock. Forlorn, they gave up and went back inside. Again the boys stayed with Emma and Nan in the girls' room all night.

The next morning when Laura was trying to wake from the drug-induced coma, Charlie Thomas gave her some more of the "medicine" to ensure she slept longer. According to Mr. Hobbs' instructions, everything had to be done without any complications or without arousing suspicion from any of the neighbors.

Charlie stomped into Nancy's room, sarcastic. "Now, how does the Queen of Hot Springs feel?" He lifted Ida up high. "I'm going to use this little one against you!" Then he chortled sadistically, a deep laugh from his belly.

"Put that baby down!" Nancy cried, but she was becoming weaker by the minute and had no strength to do anything else.

Still laughing, Charlie placed Ida back in her crib and went to check on the other men. They spent the day warming themselves up in front of the fireplace and making themselves quite at home. They stripped the shelves of anything they wanted to eat and barked orders at the children if they needed anything. Instead of making preparations for their baby sister's first birthday, the Williams children were waiting in an antechamber of hell for whatever was in store for the rest of them. Time seemed suspended, yet the sky was growing increasingly darker.

One of their neighbors and friends who had heard about their illness came and insisted on taking Ida with her to care for until the women were fully recovered. The men were in a predicament and had to give over to her demands because they did not want to arouse suspicion. Thankfully for the children, this woman unwittingly saved them when she left and carried their baby sister to her house.

Their precious grandmother had become listless in her room, and they assumed she had died. The horror was unimaginable as the children watched the monstrous mob haul another beloved member of their family out the front door and place her body inside another prepared coffin. They cried without ceasing and watched through the front window as the men rode off.

Laura finally awoke and found the children crying and looking out the living room window. Because she was still groggy, she sat down in the rocking chair. The children swarmed around her trying to explain what all had happened while she was unconscious. They informed her about their father's burial and their grandmother's death.

"Kids, Charlie wouldn't do that. He loves me." When they insisted, she began crying for her mother. "I know he did everything he could to help us, but I guess it was just too late to help your pa and grandmother." There was nothing left for the Williams children to do but grieve. Their deep sorrow enveloped the whole house, and they felt numb. Nothing could ever be any worse.

Unfortunately for the children, Charlie Thomas made his appearance again the next morning -- this time alone. George motioned for Emma and Nan, then sent them to Fletch and Mollie Jenkins' house to explain what had happened. Between sobs the girls told Mollie about their grandmother's passing. Shocked at the news of another death, Mollie packed some food and rushed to see if she could help the family.

Laura introduced her to Charlie and explained how Tom and her mother had suddenly come down sick. "Charlie gave us all some new medicine that is supposed to keep people from catching it, but I guess it was too late for them."

Charlie showed her the bottle.

She set the food on the table. "Can I have some of it? I sure don't want to catch it, either."

Charlie hesitated. "Uh, yes, you can have some."

Since he didn't know what else to do, he gave her a dose.

"Thank you, sir," she shuttered. Turning to Laura, "Well, Laura, if there is anything else I can do to help, please let me know."

"Thank you, Mollie. You've always been a dear friend."

They watched as their friend and neighbor walked out the door and disappeared. She became another victim of the evil clan when she died a couple of days later of mercuric chloride poisoning.

6

As soon as the weather cleared, Charlie rode back to Hot Springs to report the news to Mr. Hobbs. On the way there, he disposed of the bottle of poison in Buffalo Creek, the same creek where my grandfather's brother was murdered by the bushwhackers for his gold almost three decades earlier. Of course, Mr. Hobbs was ecstatic to hear the good news and praised his efforts.

They boarded an Iron Mountain Railroad car, rode over to the penitentiary in Little Rock and shared the news with the witch woman. The couple made more promises to him, but he had to complete the job to their satisfaction first. To appease him, they provided him with just enough money to do the job at hand.

When he made it back to Waldron, Charlie came to visit Laura and pressured her to marry him right away. Even though she wanted to, she felt like it was too soon and would draw criticism from the neighbors, so she made him wait for four months.

Because Charlie and Mattie Jones had taken a down-payment of a mule on the additional 40 acres that my father had purchased from them and he had not made additional payments on it due to his death, Mr. Jones was kind enough to return my father's mule to Mama.

Although I was too small to remember in detail the events that took place when I was a baby, I grew up hearing about them from my siblings, and I overheard too many things from my own mother and stepfather. When George, Dock, Emma, and Nan would be outside or visiting neighbors as they loved to do (anything to escape the predicament they found themselves in) I was that nosey child who hung on every word that passed between the adults.

I would act like I wasn't listening, but whatever I overheard compelled me to do so. It was obvious that my mother did not love her children like most mothers do because she allowed Charlie Thomas to manipulate her in every way possible, even to the detriment of her own offspring.

Some of the ladies from our church and neighborhood got word that Mama planned to marry Charlie. They were so upset about the situation and figured she was just desperate for help around the farm, so they brought a cake and came calling.

"Laura, that man is nothing but an alcoholic," Mattie Jones blurted.

"She's right, Laura. He's not fit to bring up your children," added another.

"Look, I know you ladies mean well, but my mind is made up. Besides, I love Charlie, and I do need him. He'll be fine with the children."

The stunned women looked at each other in disbelief.

"I appreciate the cake and your concern, but we *are* getting married."

The disappointed women left because they felt helpless to convince Mama otherwise, so they went and talked to William Turman about it. They knew that Laura had a lot of respect for him because he had taken her and my grandmother in and helped care for them for about ten years after my grandfather was murdered decades earlier.

It was not long until William Turman rode up in his surrey and climbed down. He counseled my mother. "Laura, you need to stop and take time before you make any rash decisions. Charlie Thomas is not going to be good for your children. Just give it some time, and you'll feel differently about things."

"I appreciate all you've done for me and Mama in the past, Mr. Turman, but I love Charlie and plan to marry him."

Disappointed, Mr. Turman hugged her. "Then I wish you all the luck, Laura. Take care of those children. You know I'll be around if there's ever anything I can do for you. You are like one of my daughters."

"Thank you, Mr. Turman. I love you, too." She watched as he climbed into his surrey and directed his horse to leave.

The wedding took place in our living room the next week. Charlie had made arrangements for a preacher to conduct the informal service. Helping himself to my father's clothes, he dressed for the occasion. My brothers and sisters were mortified. George motioned for us to come to the boys' room.

George was livid.

"That sorry piece of trash is wearing Pa's clothes!"

"I hate him!" Dock responded. Emma and Nan began crying, so I followed their lead.

"That man brought nothing with him but trouble!" George blurted. "He's even been riding Pa's horse and using his mules."

"He better not ride Salem!" Emma added.

"I saw him riding Salem yesterday," Dock replied.

About that time Charlie stuck his head in. "You kids come on. The preacher's ready." Reluctantly, we all obeyed. What else could we do? With the exception of my mother, the adults in our lives had always done the right thing for us. We were in a trap and did not have a clue how to get out.

Our lives were topsy-turvy from that moment on. We were yelled at, cursed at, and threatened if we did not do exactly as we were told, and those things escalated when Charlie was drinking. He loved taunting us and making light of the fact that he took everything our precious daddy ever owned. I guess because George was the oldest and challenged the man's authority, he caught most of the abuse. He finally had enough and ran away. We cried because we had no idea where he went. That left the four of us younger ones to catch all that Charlie could dish out.

Two years later my half-brother, Bob Thomas, was born. With his birth came the added pressure on Charlie to finish the job he had started for the witch woman and her husband. They had promised to set up trust funds for his children, even any unborn ones, if he would just get rid of the rest of Laura's heirs to the bathhouse property that was earning fortunes for them in Hot Springs.

Charlie did not waste time in pressuring Mama to put the farm up for sale. He kept promising her they would live like kings and queens if they played their cards right. Although she was reluctant at first because she was pregnant, she finally gave in after Roy was born. Charlie now had two sons of his own.

"I'll bet Mr. Turman will buy our land and all the livestock."

"Are you sure, Laura?"

"Well, he is known for buying and selling property, and he said he would help me any way he could."

"Good! I'll ride up to his place and talk to him about it."

Although Mr. Turman was a little surprised with the sudden move, he agreed to buy the 40 acres, along with the sheep, cows, hogs, and all the horses and mules except two teams and two wagons. He had no idea Charlie was planning to move us over into Oklahoma near some Indians so he and Mr. Hobbs could kill us and lay it off on the Indians. Of course, we did not know about their plan, either.

Emma found out we were moving and begged to stay with Mattie and Charlie Jones, so Mama gave her to them. She also tried to give Nan to them, but my sister cried so much, they sent her back home. Charlie was happy that he had another less Williams child to deal with, so that was fine with him. That left the three of us, along with our half-brothers, Bob and Roy Thomas, who moved over into Oklahoma.

We were supposed to meet a friend of Charlie's near an Indian settlement, so we loaded up the wagon and headed out. Traveling over Rich Mountain Pass was very rough and rocky, and the trees were short and stubby. I could not help but feel sorry for Salem and the other horses and mules because it was during the cold wintertime. When we arrived at a vacant house, Charlie informed us that it was our new house and made us help unload the wagon. I am pretty certain he never spent one penny of my father's money from the sale of his farm on the place. It appeared to have been vacated for some time. *How did he know about this house way out here?* I wondered.

While we were moving our things into the house, Charlie told Mama to start preparing supper while he went to check things out. He told us he had to look around the place because there were dangerous Indians about. I always felt safer when he was away than when he was at home. He could have been scalped by the Indians as far as I was concerned.

Unfortunately, he returned just in time for supper. He told Mama that he wanted her to send us down the road after we ate because he found another vacant house that had a nice red wagon in the yard, and he wanted us to go get it for Bob. I wondered why he didn't just bring it back himself. He also told us that Indians might kill us, but we had to go get it anyway.

Charlie said so many mean and hurtful things all the time, I did not pay much attention to that. He was nothing but a drunken old jackass who loved to hear himself bray. Also, I remember him telling Mama not to let Bob go with us because he did not want Bob to see it. Mama knew what he meant. Charlie did not want Bob to see the killings. I recall that at the time, we were just thankful when he left before we finished eating.

Mama was so superstitious about the power the witch woman had over us, she let Charlie convince her that things were for the best, even when she had reservations about doing some of them. Thankfully, I always knew that the Lord was with me and was watching over me during those terrifying times. I felt an inner peace I cannot describe.

After supper Dock, Nan, and I walked down the dirt road to the house and spotted the red wagon. There was also a shed around back. About the time we got up in the yard, we saw Charlie and another man, who we found out later was Mr. Hobbs, running toward us with axes high in the air. We flew back home to Mama who was waiting anxiously and crying. I guess the two men thought we would be easy targets.

That night was long and terrifying. Mama watched over us because she really did not have the nerve to let them go through with their plan. Mysteriously, the next morning when we all woke, there was a lot of food already on the table. Someone had brought a side of bacon and some sour kraut and left it for us. Mama said she thought it was poisoned, for us not to eat it. Even Charlie did not know about the food but suspected Mr. Hobbs of leaving it. I'm certain they were right because we looked out the front door and saw two of our horses were dead. We grieved especially for poor old Salem.

Fortunately, Mama insisted we leave and return to Arkansas. The fact that Mr. Hobbs did not warn Charlie about the poisoned food probably helped in his decision to leave when we did, so we loaded what we could and made our way back with the remaining horses and mules over Rich Mountain into the town of Mena.

7

Since we had no home to go to, we camped in a wagon yard in Mena for a few months. Life was tough for us. We children had to help with everything, and at the same time, stay out of Charlie's way. I cannot describe how degraded we felt, so unloved and unwanted, yet we had done nothing to anyone to deserve the way we were treated. Everything we did was to stay in good graces with Charlie. Even then he would make sarcastic comments and tell us our "kinfolks in Hot Springs" wanted us dead.

As far as we were concerned, we never had any relatives in Hot Springs. At least we had never met any of them. So I thought, *Why would they hate us?* According to Charlie it was because the witch woman hated our grandmother and was determined not to allow her grandchildren to have anything she ever had.

Charlie would tell Mama that Mr. and Mrs. Hobbs had nothing against her, though. That was either a lie, or he was badly mistaken. He was convinced that if he got rid of all of the Williams children that the Hobbses would just make him a partner in the bathhouse business and let Mama have half of her rightful part of it. They had promised to also set up trust funds for him and all of his children -- even any unborn ones -- and Mama somehow believed him.

How could anyone be that blind? All I can say is Charlie's mind was clouded by greed and alcohol. I cannot begin to explain Mama's issues, only that she was afraid of the witch woman and her powers over her. I never believed in witches, but oh how they worked their evil ways on my mother.

One day Charlie informed Mama that he had to make a business trip to Hot Springs, and he wanted us to all stay put. While he was away, I remember there was a big fire near our camp. Men were running and drawing water out of a well nearby, and somehow one of them fell down into the well. I was standing watching it all as frantic people were rushing to try and rescue him. Finally, they were able to get him out and finish fighting the fire.

Unfortunately, Charlie returned from Hot Springs. He came into camp laughing. "Laura, I got myself into the damndest situation."

"What was it, Charlie?" Mama was smiling at him.

"I was trying to cross the Ouachita River and drowned our damn mules," he cackled.

Those were the only two head of mules we had left from our trip to Oklahoma and back, and we children did not see the humor at all. In fact we mourned their loss. Apparently, Charlie was immune to death, even the death of human beings, so why would he care about two animals' lives?

Mama was concerned about our lack of necessities. Charlie had left her very little cash while he was away, and she needed to buy some groceries and other items.

"Charlie, we are about out of food, and we need some more supplies for camp."

"Yeah, I know we do. I'll go down to the store and get what we need. You stay here and take care of the kids. I also want to see about getting a job around here."

Although he had to still have money from the sale of my father's farm and animals, he was reluctant to give up any of that. At least if he found a job, it would keep him away from us during the day. Dock, Nan, and I were all hoping he would find one. I believe Bob and Roy felt differently about their father, but he did not treat them the same as he did us.

To our relief he found a job managing a restaurant in town. Being the manager of a popular business in town only fueled Charlie's ego, however. He strutted around like a proud peacock. His whole demeanor sickened the three of us. We never understood Mama's attraction to the man. I mean, how could she possibly think he was better than our daddy?

That summer Charlie came in from work all excited, his eyes bugged out. "Laura, that man from Hot Springs is here to fix up the papers!" He was referring to the trust fund papers. They talked awhile; although I did not hear everything that was said, I heard *plenty*. He told Mama that the man said the Williams children had to be killed before he would fix up the trust fund papers, and if they wouldn't do it, he would. Charlie was so anxious to get his hands on the money, he fully intended to go through with it.

Mama cried when he told her, but she said if it had to be done, she would do it herself. That floored me. My own mother telling this drunkard that she would kill her own children so he could have what he wanted. It was my mother's property by rights anyway. I guess she wanted it as badly as her sorry husband.

Then Charlie called me aside. He told me they were going to have to get rid of me and my brother and sister. I asked him why.

"I hate to do it, but the witch woman said it has to be done." He also added, "Your mother will get a lot of money, but you won't get any of it."

Again I asked him why.

"Because you will be dead. The only thing you will ever get will be read about in storybooks. Oh yes, you will be in storybooks."

For some unexplained reason, I was not afraid. I went out away from the camp and knelt down and prayed. I believe it was the first time I had ever really said a prayer myself. Sure, I had bowed my head before when others prayed, but this one was from my own heart and from my own lips. God heard that prayer and answered.

Apparently, Charlie had also talked to Nan because she called me aside later that evening. "Ida, come out here. I want to tell you something."

We sat down on the ground, and she wrote something with her finger in the sand. Then she spoke.

"They are going to make heirs out of Roy and Bob and kill us. Let's run away so far they can't find us."

Although we really wanted to run away as far as we could, we were little children, 8 and 10 years-old, and had no clue where that would be. I am sure Nan had regrets about crying so much at Mattie Jones' house that they had to bring her back home; however, she was the only sister I had left in the world, and I don't know what I would have done without her. We became inseparable after all we had been through together.

Mama watched all night with a gun in her hands. I never could figure her out. It seemed at times she actually cared about us, then other times she did not. It was in those rare instances when her motherly instincts seemed to make an appearance that I had temporary feelings of compassion for her. (Yes, I actually felt sorry for her at times.)

Hobbs hired a lawyer by the name of George
Donaghey. (It is a distinct probability that he was the
same man who just a few years later was elected as
governor of Arkansas) to draw up the trust fund
papers on the bathhouse property at Hot Springs, so
Hobbs had Charlie force Mama to sign a will to be
filed with those papers.

There were four trust funds set up. There were
three small ones and one large one. The large one
was 75 per cent, and it was called the Baby Fund.
One of the small ones was for Bob, the second was for
Roy, and the third was for my sister, Mary Emily
(Emma.) Their plan was to kill Dock, Nan, and me,
but they knew if they claimed Emma was dead that
Charlie and Mattie Jones, who were caring for her,
would not lie for them, so they were forced to set up
one for her. The last thing they wanted was for the
law to be after them.

Sometime later we were being hauled off down
the road in the back of our wagon toward the Catholic
school so we could camp there near a running creek.
I saw Charlie point out toward the fields and heard
him say, "Laura, hadn't you rather see them buried
out yonder than scattered all over the world?"
Obviously, he either did not know I was listening, or
he did not care if I heard him. All I can say is my
guardian angel saved me. Whenever I was feeling
lonely and sad, I always felt his presence.

Arriving at the Catholic school was one of a very few pleasant experiences for us. The nuns there were very helpful and friendly. They gladly helped the two of us sisters carry buckets of water from the creek that flowed close to the camp where we stayed, and they always had pleasant things to say to us children. They also enjoyed talking with Dock and helping in any way they could. We were so unaccustomed to people talking to us like we had any importance or like our words had any merit to them. They actually made us feel significant in this world.

One morning Charlie took Bob and Roy to have their pictures made to be filed with the papers. Roy had on a flowered dress, and both boys were barefooted and wore hats. Since I really wanted my picture made also, I asked if he would have mine made. He spouted off, "I don't need your picture made, only Bob and Roy's." Another nail in my coffin of self-esteem.

Later Mama's half-brother, Moses, the same one married to the witch-woman's daughter, Mary Hobbs, came to the camp and talked privately with her. He just looked curiously at me but did not say a word. I was puzzled by him and did not have a good feeling. If he was related, why would he just stare at me like that?

Another morning later on, Charlie grabbed Dock. "Tell them all goodbye. It will be the last time you will see them." He turned toward Mama. "I'm taking Dock off to kill him."

Why Mama put up with that I will never understand. She could have had the law help us out, I believe.

Instead she cried. "Oh, my poor Dock, my poor boy!" Then we watched as Charlie put him in the wagon and rode off. We cried all day, and Mama said he was her father's namesake, too. His name was William Hamilton Williams, named after our grandfather. In those days a lot of folks had more than one name, and many had nicknames.

Late that evening Charlie rode up. Anxious, I asked him where Dock was. He laughed and said he had gotten away from him and Hobbs. Apparently, he had made plans to meet Hobbs and kill my brother.

"He ran like a spotted ape!" he blurted.

It infuriated me to hear him call my sweet brother a spotted ape. He also told us that he found out George had been killed. We cried all night for him. That was another long, terrifying night for Nan and me. The two of us knew we were next on their twisted agenda.

The following day we were guarded closely. Charlie wanted to make sure we did not talk to the nuns about anything we had heard. When it was getting late he called all of us out to see the sunset in front of the camp. I will never forget his callous words directed to my sister and me.

"You two look at the sunset for your last time." He talked freely about all of the things that had happened. I guess he figured we would not live to tell anyone about them, so he held nothing back. Also, he instructed my mother not to ever tell their children (Bob and Roy) what caused the deaths of their grandmother and Mama's first husband.

"Laura, I want you to get up early in the morning and get the girls ready. Mr. Hobbs will be out there waiting on us."

Even though we had seen Hobbs over in Oklahoma, we did not realize who he was, so that name meant nothing to Nan and me at the time. Charlie usually referred to him as "the man from Hot Springs" around us.

At the crack of dawn the next morning Mama instructed Nan and me to put on our very best dresses. She also had us wear our bonnets. I was hoping we were going to get our pictures made or go to church, but that was not their plan. Charlie told us we were going to hunt chestnuts. I never knew we had any chestnuts around and had never seen any before. Of course, they left Bob and Roy in the care of someone else before we left.

Many times before Charlie had made the remarks to me that he was keeping me to pull the chestnuts out of the fire for him, so I really paid no attention to it. There were so many ridiculous comments that had come out of his mouth, I just figured he was drunk. He had told me more than once that the little witch trick worked; that they had me in a big boiling pot with my legs sticking out.

Another time he told me that he was the monkey, and I was the cat. "The monkey takes the cat and makes her take her paw and pull out the nuts that had roasted in the fire." As far as I was concerned, he was the only nut around.

Charlie, Mama, Nan and I began walking. They gave us baskets to carry and told us to run ahead and look for chestnuts. Not realizing our danger, we just enjoyed the outing by running from bush to bush. Of course there were no chestnuts in the area, but we did not know that. It is amazing how badly children want to trust those in charge of them.

We walked on for miles before we saw a man coming toward us. Mama was frightened, so Charlie told her, "Don't be afraid, Laura; he won't hurt you."

I asked what the man was doing there, and my stepfather told me he was looking for a pot of gold. When we got closer, we realized it was the same man we had seen over in Oklahoma at the vacant house. Charlie introduced him to Mama. "This is my wife, and I did what I told you I would do. I told you I would get her, didn't I?"

They talked for a while, then Hobbs reached out to grab Nan's and my hands. Because he was looking so mean at us and we remembered him being the same man with the ax, we were afraid and jumped back behind Mama.

Charlie asked her, "Laura, do you think you can go through with it?"

"Yes."

Then Charlie told Mr. Hobbs, "That is all right Mr. Hobbs; we will do it ourselves." The two men seemed more excited than Mama; she seemed the calmest of the three.

Our parents led us farther up the road with Mr. Hobbs following at a distance. When we came upon an old mine shaft or cave, we stopped. Charlie took Nan's hand and led her inside. It was only a few minutes before Nan darted back outside toward us all excited.

"What are they doing with those knives in there?"

Charlie came out and told Mama to hold Nancy. Then he grabbed my hand and led me inside. There was a board shelf with three or four butcher knives laying on it. If I live to be one hundred, I will never forget his words.

"I am going to cut your little throat. Pick out the knife you want me to use."

I pointed to the shiniest knife and said, "I guess that one will do." For some reason I was calm and asked him why he was going to kill me.

"Because your kinfolks in Hot Springs want you killed. You don't know them, but they know you."

He looked so strangely at me and started shaking, as if he could not bring himself to follow through. Either it was because I was so calm and was staring straight into his eyes, or it was because he actually had compassion for children since he had two of his own.

For whatever reason, he said he just could not do it and laid the knife down and let go of me. I darted out the opening and hid with Nancy behind Mama. She seemed relieved. Hobbs was out away near some trees, looking on.

Charlie came out of the cave. "Laura, I will wait here. You take your girls and have your last walk together." Then he pointed in the direction he wanted us to go.

The area was beautiful, and Mama began to cry. I asked her why she was crying, but she did not answer. We continued our walk until we came to a muddy area with tall, slender grass growing all around it. When we stopped to look around, I somehow felt the presence of angels. The sun was shining brightly over the spot.

Charlie showed up from behind. He took off our bonnets and laid them on the ground. Then he started to pick me up in order to throw me in, but he changed his mind. Pointing out over the pit, he instructed Nan and me. "You girls hold hands and jump as far as you can that way."

Mama turned around and covered her face. I started to jump in in order to please him, but Nan yanked me back. "Watch out! That is a bog hole." I had not realized we were standing in front of a quicksand pit.

About that time I looked up and saw four forms coming toward me. It was my grandfather, my grandmother, and what appeared to be two angel babies with wings. I yelled out, "There is Grandma!" The others could not see her because she had been dead for several years. This seemed to have spooked the men because Hobbs and my stepfather walked off a little ways and talked. On his way back I saw Charlie pick up a fence rail and throw it in the bog hole. It went almost out of sight. Apparently, my vision had an impact on their decision because Charlie and Hobbs told Mama that they would let us go if she would just sign papers saying the girls had died.

"Will you sign them?" Hobbs asked.

"Yes, I'll sign the damn papers!" Mama retorted.

The men seemed pleased and relieved at the same time. Mr. Hobbs left us there and went back to Mena to have the papers drawn up by a lawyer.

Charlie found a place with a huge rock and told Nan and me to hide behind it until dark because he did not want anyone to see us because they were going to file a report that we had died.

"From now on you girls will have new names. You can never use your real names again. Ida, your new name will be 'Bunch.'" [I hated that name, but that is what I was called for many years afterward.] "Nancy, you will be called 'Nan' from now on." [Her shortened name stuck for the rest of her life.]

They left us there all by ourselves until dark. We were all alone and afraid, but I know the Lord was watching over us and was our comforter. Mama and Charlie finally showed back up in a wagon, and we camped there for the night.

Nan and I found out the next morning that Mama had made arrangements to leave us at the McDonald farm just outside town, so she and Charlie and their boys could meet Hobbs at the lawyer's office and sign the papers swearing that four of us Williams children were found dead. They could not include Emma's name because she was living with the Joneses back in Waldron.

Spending the day with Mrs. McDonald and her children was such a pleasant experience. It was one of such a few fun childhood memories that we had. We played all day like normal girls do. At least that is how I envisioned normal children playing with no real concerns on their minds. As far as Nan and I were concerned, we could have stayed with the McDonald family for the rest of our lives. They all seemed to have really enjoyed us being there and worked hard to make us feel welcome and at home. We felt as if someone had removed boulders off of our shoulders.

Of course our reprieve was shattered when Hobbs rode up in a wagon and tried to get Nan and me to climb on and leave with him. "Come and get in the wagon. I won't hurt you much." We refused, so he scolded us for ignoring him.

Fortunately, Mrs. McDonald saw what was happening and came to investigate. Hobbs saw her, introduced himself, and politely explained that he was a relative of ours and was supposed to pick us up and take us home. Our body language told her otherwise.

"No, sir, their parents left them in my charge. They will stay with me until their parents pick them up." We could not have been more relieved.

Unfortunately, Mama and Charlie returned in their wagon to get us. They thanked Mrs. McDonald for watching us for the day.

"Oh, we really enjoyed their company. I know the kids had a good time playing together. It's not often we have visitors."

Charlie instructed the horses to leave. As we rode back toward Mena, I reflected on all that had happened to my siblings and me. I wondered how George had died, and I wondered what had happened to Dock. Even though I knew where Emma was and figured she was fine, I still missed her. My heart was heavy, and I wondered what lay in store for Nan and me. The outlook seemed bleak.

About the time we were passing an open field, I looked up in the sky and saw my grandmother once again. This time she was alone. There was no one else around her. I waved at her. Tears began streaming down my face. How I missed that sweet lady, the only woman in my life that really loved and cared for me and my siblings.

Nan and Ida Williams
Cherry Hill, Arkansas
1900

8

When we arrived back in Mena, Hobbs told Charlie to take us over to Cherry Hill and join the Masonic Lodge there. He admitted that if anything ever came up about the incident in Mena, the Masons would help him get out of it. Charlie did move us to Cherry Hill and joined the Masonic Lodge, but he messed around and got himself into trouble with someone there, so their little plan disintegrated.

Cherry Hill is a very small town just a few miles from Mena. My stepfather took a job there overseeing a cotton gin, forming cotton into bales to be shipped to other parts of the world. That was about 1900. We children enjoyed playing around that large gin and around the gristmill located nearby.

Watching corn being ground into meal and wheat into flour was interesting. It was one of the few things we enjoyed doing. It was during those years that Nan and I began forming a bond with our half-brothers. After all, they were innocent little fellows and could not help the fact that their father was just a cow patty covered in blow-flies on the trail -- no more than we could help the fact that our own mother was an unfit parent. None of us children had asked to be conceived nor had we asked our parents to behave in the manner in which they had chosen.

The following spring my baby half-sister, Era Thomas, was born. She was named after the *Hot Springs New Era* newspaper and would have been an heir for the Baby Fund if she had lived to adulthood. She was such a sweet little girl, unselfish, but she was too good to live in this old world. She never got to see her third birthday before the Lord took her.

It seemed that Charlie had begun to soften his attitude toward us over the years. He even took Nan and me into Cherry Hill and had our picture made. Years earlier he had warned me never to go to Hot Springs, even 50 years later, or my relatives there would kill me. Now he was telling me he wished we could all go up there and they could watch us kids grow up with the town; however, Mr. Hobbs had told him never to bring us there. He later told Charlie to move us out of Arkansas completely.

My stepfather even joked about putting me in a box and dropping me in the Ouachita River and letting the river deliver me to them at Hot Springs. When I told him the river did not run up the mountain, we both laughed about it. For the first time I saw my stepfather as a human being with feelings for others.

One day he was reading the newspaper and laughed. There was an article stating that the Blackwell grandchildren's bodies had never been found. I never will forget that day and what he said.

"Bunch, you are one of them, and the boys are out in the mountains looking for you."

I wish I could remember if it was in the *Mena Evening Star* or a Hot Springs newspaper, but I do remember picking it up and looking at it.

Charlie told me that when I was old enough, to write a postal card to the Mena Evening Star and tell them to publish an article saying that I was not dead. But he also warned me not to ever mention about the property in Hot Springs, or he would get into trouble over it. Well, I grew up and forgot all about writing them.

However, I was able to find out that both of my brothers and Emma were living and doing well. George had made his way over into Oklahoma and was living there. When Dock had escaped the clutches of our stepdad and Mr. Hobbs that fateful day, he bolted as fast as he could until he came to an abrupt halt at the sight of a kind old black man riding in a wagon. Thankfully, the man took him into town. Dock first made his way to George Rose's in Boles but somehow ended up later in Portales, New Mexico, where he became a well-known horse fancier.

When I talked with George, he told me that he had made a trip to Hot Springs in 1904 to see about the property. That is when he came face-to-face with Mr. Hobbs, who threatened to kill him if he did not leave town. Since he did not know what else to do, he returned to Oklahoma.

Charlie told us later that Mr. Hobbs died in 1908. His wife, the witch woman, lived to be 88 years old where she died in prison. I guess they both finally received retribution for their dastardly deeds. Although I'm not sure, I feel certain Mr. Hobbs had initially sent Charlie down to meet my mother and convince her to marry him when I was very small. I find it too coincidental that Charlie was in cahoots with Mr. Hobbs up in Hot Springs and just happened to show up next door to us and got involved with Mama.

My mother and stepfather had another daughter, Hallie Thomas, but they eventually separated, and he moved down into Texas. He was killed in the 1915 hurricane at La Porte. Whether he ever repented of his sins, I do not know.

When I was well into adulthood, I did make a trip to Hot Springs myself to try and find out information about my grandparents' land. From what I understand, it ran the length of where "Bathhouse Row" and the Quapaw Bathhouse now stands. However, years before, the government had come in and had taken claim of all of the properties in that area. (At least I hope the Hobbses lost their control over it and stopped getting rich from it.) We never got so much as a bath out of it.

In 1939 I heard many reports on the radio about the funds. Mama was in poor health and living with me and my family at the time. As little as she had done for us when I was growing up, I felt it was my duty to take care of her in her old age. One report said the Baby Fund had grown so big that there was talk of putting some of it into the three smaller funds.

Mama and I were listening to one of the reports, and we heard the Cummins' daughter, the Little Rock Heiress, the one who had played with Mama at the resort when they were little, trying to find "the Crying Heiress of Hot Springs" to help her get her property. Mama said she remembered her and that she herself was "the Crying Heiress." We knew then that the woman was trying to get in touch with my mother; however, Mama never did anything about it. I guess she figured it was futile.

As far as I know, my mother never apologized to any of us for the things she allowed to go on when we were children. She took those things with her to her grave in 1946.

When I was 22 years-old, I went to visit Nan in DeRidder, Louisiana. That is when I met and eventually married Joseph Middleton Higginbotham, and together we have raised five sons and one daughter. Unfortunately, our first daughter, Ethel, died at birth. Due to the Great Depression and WWII, our lives have been extremely difficult. However, those are two separate stories in themselves.

When the doctor mistakenly diagnosed Joseph with tuberculosis, he advised us to move to Colorado. It was there he was hired for the railroad. After the company laid off workers, we moved to Houston, and he worked at the creosote company here. He constructed our house and our outhouses until he finally installed plumbing. Also, he grew most of our food in our gardens, which he tended for years; and we never went hungry.

Our four oldest boys, Marvin, Merrion, Murphy, and Milton served our country during WWII. Marvin was a gunnery instructor; Merrion was a fighter pilot who flew 33 missions over Hitler's Germany and who was shot down in France but survived; Murphy was a Ranger who fought and was wounded in the D-Day invasion but survived gangrene thanks to the discovery of penicillin, and Milton was a radioman in the Pacific aboard a ship. Our only surviving daughter, Mildred, became a well-known real estate broker in the Houston and NASA area. Our youngest son, Maurice, became a telegrapher first for the Santa Fe and later for the Houston Belt & Terminal Railroad.

If there was a way to help my children or grandchildren, as far as receiving anything from what was supposed to have been our properties, I would do so, but I am an old woman now and do not see that happening. I have done everything I know and have thought to do. However, I know that our lives are more important than all the riches this old world has to offer, and I will stand before the Lord one day and have a clear conscience about it all.

Home at waldron   aug. 22 1944

waldron Scott Co. ark. was where we lived when
our own Father and Grandmother was living.
Grandmother Blackwell lived at our house. we
had a fine lady and a darling Grandmother, and
she loved us very much and our home was
a happy home and lots of friends at waldron
our parents own 40 acres about one mile from waldron
our Father, Thomas H. williams better known as
"Tom" williams bought the land from Tom Bates he had
that land payed for and a house on it, and then he
bought 40 acres of land from charley and mattie
Jones and payed the first down payment on the
land by leting him mr Jones have a mule for the
payment and our lady died before he made any
more payments mr Jones then mr Jones brought
the mule back to our mother but do own the land
the land from Jones, but do own the land
from mr. Bates our mother said the land was
not much good but it had a lot of black
walnut trees on it but I have heard that
the trees was all cut and moved a way and
the house our father built had burned down
many years after & we left there.
our Father and Grandmother was buried not far from
where we lived in Squire Rock grave yard there
was never any markers put on their graves you see
we were all little kids then and couldn't do anything
if we was den in posision to it will go back and
have tumstones put on their graves I have all way
wanted to do that for my lady and some day it
hope I can go back

olie

ABOUT THE AUTHOR

Vivian Nichols is a retired English teacher who lives in Palestine, Texas with Gary, her husband of 43 years. Their three children, Jared, Crystal, and Seth, along with their spouses, have blessed them with nine grandchildren. A deep Christian faith and their love for music are two important aspects of their lives. They also love to travel. She has authored four other books.

Made in the USA
San Bernardino, CA
18 November 2017